TRIVIA FOR SMART KIDS

300+ Questions About Sports, History, Food, Fairy Tales, and So Much More

Cooper the Pooper

© **Copyright 2021 Cooper The Pooper - All rights reserved.**

The content contained within this book may not be reproduced, duplicated or transmitted without direct written permission from the author or the publisher.

Under no circumstances will any blame or legal responsibility be held against the publisher, or author, for any damages, reparation or monetary loss due to the information contained within this book, either directly or indirectly.

Legal Notice:
This book is copyright protected. It is only for personal use. You cannot amend, distribute, sell, use, quote or paraphrase any part, or the content within this book, without the consent of the author or publisher.

Disclaimer Notice:
Please note the information contained within this document is for educational and entertainment purposes only. All effort has been executed to present accurate, up to date, reliable, complete information. No warranties of any kind are declared or implied. Readers acknowledge that the author is not engaged in the rendering of legal, financial, medical or professional advice. The content within this book has been derived from various sources. Please consult a licensed professional before attempting any techniques outlined in this book.

By reading this document, the reader agrees that under no circumstances is the author responsible for any losses, direct or indirect, that are incurred as a result of the use of the information contained within this document, including, but not limited to, errors, omissions or inaccuracies.

TABLE OF CONTENTS

Introduction 4

Chapter 1: Animals 6

Chapter 2: Space 18

Chapter 3: Geography 30

Chapter 4: Sports 44

Chapter 5: History 56

Chapter 6: Food 68

Chapter 7: Nature 80

Chapter 8: Movies 94

Chapter 9: Fairy Tales 106

Final Words 120

INTRODUCTION

Do you like knowing about *stuff*?

I mean, did you know that butterflies taste with their feet? What about that a full NASA space suit costs a whopping 12 million dollars?

Or that on a yearly basis, cows kill more people than sharks do?

Well prepare to be amazed!

See, in your hands you have a book full of more than 300 amazing trivia questions. Trivia questions about animals, bugs, nature, math, movies, and pretty much anything else you can think of.

In fact, I would go as far to say that this is probably the largest collection of trivia questions on the planet.

And definitely the largest written by a dog.

See, once upon a time, I spent all my time lying in the sun, digging through the trash, and playing games with the neighborhood kids.

But then, over time, the neighborhood kids stopped coming out so much.

To be honest, they hardly came out at all.

Instead, they started spending all their time playing silly little games on their phone.

Seriously, could you get any more boring?

And just like that I decided that something needed to change.

So, I started writing books.

But not just any old books mind you. Books that you can share with your friends and your family. Books that get you having a heap of fun.

And what better option than trivia questions!

With that in mind, I travelled the world looking for some of the best trivia questions I could find. Then, once I had found them all, I created this amazing book.

If you are after some ridiculous trivia questions to share with your friends and family, look no further because I have got you covered.

Dive on in and prepare to laugh, cry, and giggle yourself into a world of trivia silliness.

01

How many legs does an octopus have?
A) Nine
B) Eight
C) Five
D) Six

Answer: B.
Octopi have eight slimy tentacles that are used for moving underwater and to catch prey.

02

What is a baby kangaroo called?
A) Puppy
B) Doe
C) Joey
D) Roo

Answer: C.
A kangaroo baby is called a joey and can weigh less than a gram at birth, measuring only about two centimeters long.

03

Which animal does not drink water?
A) Sloth
B) Reindeer
C) Fish
D) Kangaroo rat

Answer: D.
Kangaroo rats live in hot, dry areas; therefore, they conserve water from the seeds they eat and do not drink water.

04

What is the largest mammal in the world?
A) Elephant
B) Giraffe
C) Blue whale
D) Hippopotamus

Answer: C.
The blue whale is the largest mammal in the world and can weigh around 110,231 to 330,694 pounds.

05

What food do panda bears eat?
A) Grass
B) Bamboo
C) Insects
D) Ants

Answer: B.
A panda bear can eat 20 to 40 pounds of delicious bamboo stalks every day.

06

What kind of animal is a Komodo dragon?
A) Lizard
B) Dragon
C) Snake
D) Bird

Answer: A.
Komodo dragons are lizards, but they are called dragons because of their massive size and their dragon-like faces.

07
A snail can sleep for how many years?
A) Two years
B) Three years
C) 100 years
D) even years

Answer: B.
Snails can sleep for three years when the environment is too hot or dry to survive.

08
How many bones do sharks have?
A) 305
B) 255
C) Zero
D) 98

Answer: C.
Shark bodies do not have any bones, as the shark skeleton is made of only cartilage.

09
What is the tallest animal in the world?
A) Ostrich
B) Giraffe
C) Deer
D) Duck

Answer: B.
Giraffes are the tallest animals in the world. The giraffe neck can grow to almost eight feet long.

10
What animal is the slowest in the world?
A) Three-toed sloth
B) Snail
C) Tortoise
D) Turtle

Answer: A.
The three-toed sloth is so slow that it travels only 41 yards per day, almost half the length of a football field.

11

What is rhino horn made out of?
A) Iron
B) Hair
C) Calcium
D) Bone

Answer: B.
Rhino horn is made from keratin, a type of fiber which is found in hair and fingernails. When a rhino horn is polished, it turns clear and shiny.

12

What is the smallest reptile in the world?
A) Chameleon
B) Lizard
C) Gecko
D) Frog

Answer: A.
The leaf chameleon can grow to around 0.5 inches, which makes it small enough to sit on the head of a match.

13

What animal can rotate its head 270 degrees?
A) Chameleon
B) Owl
C) Cat
D) Chicken

Answer: B.
An owl can rotate its head 270 degrees without breaking blood vessels or tearing tendons.

14

What is the fastest mammal on land?
A) Hare
C) Cheetah
B) Alligator
D) Eagle

Answer: C.
A cheetah can reach speeds of about 93 miles per hour while chasing prey.

15

What African animal's name means "water horse?"
A) Manatee
C) Horse
B) Hippopotamus
D) Whale

Answer: B.
Hippopotamus means "water horse" because hippos are related to horses and they enjoy wading in water.

16

What is the only bird that can fly backward?
A) Finch
C) Seagull
B) Eagle
D) Hummingbird

Answer: D.
Hummingbirds can fly backward, from side to side, and they are capable of hovering.

17

How many compartments does a cow's stomach have?
A) One
C) Four
B) Two
D) Seven

Answer: C.
Cows have four compartments in their stomachs to allow tougher food to be broken down.

18

What animal is a Portuguese man-of-war?
A) Fish
B) Jellyfish
C) Bird
D) Soldier

Answer: B.
A Portuguese man-of-war is a jellyfish with a head that floats above the surface of the water, resembling an old warship sailing.

19

What animal uses echolocation (sound waves) to move around in the dark?
A) Whale
B) Bat
C) Bird
D) Fish

Answer: B.
Bats use echolocation to find hard surfaces, predators, and prey in the dark.

20

Which are the only two mammals that lay legs?
A) Fish and bird
B) The Komodo dragon and an anaconda
C) The spiny anteater and the duck-billed platypus
D) The great eagle and a vulture

Answer: C.
Only the spiny anteater and the duck-billed platypus are mammals that lay eggs to reproduce.

21

What animal has rectangular pupils?
A) Cow
B) Horse
C) Goat
D) Donkey

Answer: C.
Rectangular pupils allow the goat to have a wider range of sight, to protect them from predators.

22

What animal is the largest rodent?
A) Rat
B) Capybara
C) Mouse
D) Squirrel

Answer: B.
A capybara weighs around 77-145.5 pounds and is around 3.6-4.3 feet long.

23

What animals can sleep for up to 22 hours each day?
A) Koala bear
B) Brown bear
C) Grizzly bear
D) Polar bear

Answer: A.
Koala bears eat eucalyptus leaves which need a lot of sleep to digest.

24

What is Scotland's national animal?

A) Mermaid
B) Unicorn
C) Leprechauns
D) None of the above

Answer: B.
Scotland is popular for its myths and legends, and therefore, the unicorn is the Scottish national animal.

25

A troglodyte is an animal that can only survive in what habitat?

A) Tundra
B) Forests
C) Caves
D) Underwater

Answer: C.
Troglodytes have special adaptations that only allow them to survive in cave habitats.

26

What does an iguana have three of?

A) Eyes
B) Hearts
C) Lungs
D) Feet

Answer: A.
The iguana's 3rd eye is on the animal's forehead, and it is used to control body temperature and sleep patterns.

27

What animal has a pregnancy period of only 12 days?
A) Whale
B) Kangaroo
C) Human being
D) Opossum

Answer: D.
Each opossum is pregnant for 12 days and can have up to 20 babies.

28

How many pairs of eyelids do owls have?
A) Three
B) Five
C) Seven
D) One

Answer: A.
All three eyelids are used to protect and clean the owl's eyes.

29

Other than humans, which is the only primate capable of having blue-colored eyes?
A) Chimpanzee
B) Monkey
C) Black lemur
D) Gorilla

Answer: C.
A black lemur is capable of having blue eyes, which lack pigment.

30

What is the only animal with an odd number of whiskers?
A) Catfish
B) Tiger
C) Rabbit
D) Mouse

Answer: A.
A catfish is the only animal to naturally have an odd number of whiskers.

31

What species of bird eats bones?
A) Eagle
B) Bearded vulture
C) Pigeon
D) Seagull

Answer: B.
Bearded vultures are scavengers; therefore, they eat the leftovers and bones left by other predators.

32

Which is the only snake that builds a nest?
A) Anaconda
B) Viper
C) King cobra
D) All of the above

Answer: C.
A king cobra is the only snake that builds a nest in order to sleep and lay eggs.

33

What continent are chinchillas from?
A) South America
B) North America
C) Asia
D) Africa

Answer: A.
Chinchillas are native to South America, and long-tailed chinchillas are an endangered species.

34

How many eyes do most spiders have?
A) Two
B) Four
C) Six
D) Eight

Answer: D.
Spiders usually have eight eyes: two very large front eyes to get a clear, color image and judge distance, and extra side eyes to detect when something is moving.

35

An ant says, "Danger ahead!" by doing what?
A) Squealing
B) Running toward water
C) Rolling on its back
D) Oozing chemicals

Answer: D.
Ants warn other ants of danger with chemical signals.

36

Which of the following is NOT a type of penguin?
A) Waterland
B) Emperor
C) Chinstrap
D) Macaroni

Answer: A.
Waterland. Emperor, Chinstrap, and Macaroni penguins are three of the 18 different species of penguin whereas Waterland is NOT a type of penguin.

01

Which of the eight planets is the fastest planet?
A) Jupiter
B) Mercury
C) Venus
D) Mars

Answer: B.
Mercury is the fastest planet as it rotates around the sun at 393,701 feet per hour.

02

What planet is known for the Great Red Spot?
A) Saturn
B) Mercury
C) Jupiter
D) Uranus

Answer: C.
Jupiter's Great Red Spot is an area of the planet that is always at high-pressure, which produces a cyclonic storm.

03

What planet is covered by mostly water?
A) Mars
B) Venus
C) Jupiter
D) Earth

Answer: D.
Earth is covered by 71% water and 29% land.

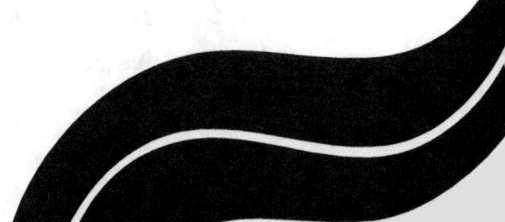

04
Which is the largest moon in the solar system?
A) Titan
B) Cyclops
C) The Moon
D) The Giant Moon

Answer: A.
Titan is the largest moon in the solar system, and it is present in Saturn's atmosphere.

05
What is the highest peak on Mars called?
A) The High Peak
B) The Alps
C) Kilimanjaro
D) Olympus Mons

Answer: D.
Olympus Mons is the highest peak on Mars, measuring around 82,021 feet high.

06
How long does it take Neptune to orbit around the sun once?
A) 1,000 years
B) 150 years
C) 165 years
D) 55 years

Answer: C.
Neptune takes 165 years to orbit the sun once.

07

What spacecraft is currently watching over Jupiter?
A) Mars
B) Juno
C) Ares
D) Hera

Answer: B.
Juno is a spacecraft orbiting Jupiter so that scientists can learn more about the planet.

08

Which of the eight planets has the same name as the Roman God of the Sea?
A) Jupiter
B) Neptune
C) Saturn
D) Uranus

Answer: B.
The planet Neptune has the same name as the Roman God of the Sea because of its blue color, which looks like the ocean.

09

Which planet could become a new human habitat?
A) Mars
B) Uranus
C) Venus
D) Mercury

Answer: A.
Mars has good water content and an atmosphere almost like Earth; therefore, Mars could be a new human habitat.

10
Which planet is named after the Roman Goddess of Beauty?
A) Venus
B) Jupiter
C) Saturn
D) Mercury

Answer: A.
Venus is named after the Roman Goddess of Beauty because it shines brighter than the other planets.

11
Which of the eight planets is the hottest planet in the solar system?
A) Venus
B) Earth
C) Mercury
D) Mars

Answer: A.
Although Mercury is closer to the sun than Venus, Venus is the hottest planet as the gases in the atmosphere trap heat.

12
Which of the eight planets is the closest planet to the sun?
A) Mercury
B) Venus
C) Earth
D) Mars

Answer: A.
Mercury is the first planet in our solar system, and it is closest to the sun.

13

What planet is famous for the pretty rings that float around it?

A) Saturn
B) Neptune
C) Jupiter
D) Mars

Answer: A.
Saturn has eight rings around it that are made of dust and gases.

14

What organization uses telescopes and science equipment to learn more about space and the planets?

A) Dunkin' Donuts
B) NASA
C) The Space Company
D) Science World

Answer: B.
NASA stands for National Aeronautics and Space Administration.

15

What is NASA's most famous space telescope?

A) The Wobble
B) Wonder Space Telescope
C) The Shuffle Shuttle
D) The Hubble Space Telescope

Answer: D.
The Hubble Telescope is now 340 miles above the earth's surface, and it completes 15 orbits per day.

16

Who was the first person to walk on the moon?
A) Arthur Pendragon
B) Buzz Lightyear
C) Neil Armstrong
D) None of the above

Answer: C.
On the 20th of July 1969, Neil Armstrong was the first human being to set foot on the moon.

17

What force keeps the earth orbiting the sun?
A) Balance
B) Friction
C) Gravity
D) All of the above

Answer: C.
Gravity is the force of the sun that keeps the earth in orbit.

18

What are the deep holes in the moon called?
A) Pits
B) Holes
C) Craters
D) Boulders

Answer: C.
A crater is a bowl-shaped hole in the ground that is hollow and is caused by a meteorite or explosion.

19 What do we call man-made objects that orbit Earth and track the weather?
A) Space stations
B) Shuttles
C) Weather satellites
D) None of the above

Answer: C.
Weather satellites are large machines that circle the earth and track the weather on Earth.

20 What is a meteor called when it falls to Earth?
A) Comet
B) Meteorite
C) Shower
D) Rock

Answer: B.
A meteorite is a large piece of rock from a comet or asteroid that falls to Earth.

21 What is the name of our galaxy?
A) Kit-Kat
B) Mars
C) The Solar System
D) The Milky Way

Answer: D.
Our galaxy is called the Milky Way because it looks like a milky band of light from a distance.

22 A light-year is a measure of:
A) Time
B) Distance
C) Radiation
D) Weight

Answer: B.
A light-year is the measure of distance in space.

23

How many stars are in the Big Dipper?
A) One
B) Seven
C) 10
D) 23

Answer: B.
The Big Dipper is a constellation of stars in our galaxy made of seven bright stars.

24

How long does it take the moon to circle the earth?
A) A year
B) About 28 days
C) 24 hours
D) A week

Answer: C.
The moon makes a complete circle around the earth every 24 hours, meaning after one day.

25

Which object used to be a planet orbiting the sun, but is no longer?
A) Pluto
B) Saturn
C) An asteroid
D) Jupiter

Answer: A.
Pluto used to be considered a planet in our solar system; however, it has no longer been considered a planet since 2006.

26

What do we call the sun and all the planets orbiting it?
A) The galaxy
B) The universe
C) The solar system
D) None of the above

Answer: C.
The solar system is made of the sun and the eight planets, with moons.

27

Where is the coldest place in the universe?
A) The Boomerang Nebula
B) The Ocean
C) Mount Everest
D) Jupiter

Answer: A.
The Boomerang Nebula is one degree Kelvin (equal to -272.15 degrees Celsius) and is the coldest place in the universe.

28

How many planets are in the solar system?
A) Eight
B) Six
C) Three
D) Five

Answer: A.
There are eight planets in the solar system.

29
Which was the first manned NASA space flight to the moon?
A) Apollo 17
B) Sputnik
C) Apollo 8
D) Frederick 34

Answer: A.
Apollo 17 launched in December 1972 as the first space launch by NASA.

30
How many moons are there in our solar system?
A) Five
B) One
C) 181
D) 27

Answer: C.
There are 181 moons in our solar system with different sizes and quantities per planet.

31
Which planet is known as the red planet?
A) Venus
B) Mars
C) Jupiter
D) Saturn

Answer: B.
The planet Mars is called the red planet because it is red-colored due to the iron minerals in the rock.

32
What is the sun?
A) Star
B) Planet
C) Rock
D) Volcano

Answer: A.
The sun is a star because it makes its own energy.

33

What planet do the moons Oberon and Titania belong to?
A) Uranus
B) Jupiter
C) Venus
D) Earth

Answer: A.
Oberon and Titania are two of Uranus's 27 moons.

34

What Italian astronomer was the first to study the stars through a telescope?
A) Newton
B) Galileo
C) Einstein
D) Darwin

Answer: B.
Galileo was the first one who used the telescope for astronomy, making wonderful discoveries about our moon, the moons of Jupiter, and other things.

35

Shooting stars are actually what?
A) Comets
B) Satellites
C) Meteors
D) Asteroids

Answer: C.
A "falling star" or a "shooting star" has nothing at all to do with a star! These amazing streaks of light you can sometimes see in the night sky are caused by tiny bits of dust and rock called "meteors."

01

Which is the tallest mountain on Earth?
A) Mount Washington
B) Mount Whitney
C) Mount Everest
D) Mount St. Helens

Answer: C.
Mount Everest is in Asia and it is the tallest mountain in the world. It measures around 29,000 feet above sea level.

02

How many deserts are there in Africa?
A) Eight
B) Seven
C) Four
D) Three

Answer: D.
Africa has three deserts: the Sahara, Kalahari, and Namib.

03

Which is the largest North American Great Lake?
A) Lake Superior
B) Lake Scary
C) Lake Erie
D) Lake Gargantuan

Answer: A.
Lake Superior is the largest of the five Great Lakes on and near the border between Canada and the United States. The other lakes are Lake Huron, Lake Erie, Lake Ontario, and Lake Michigan.

04

Which of the following places is not a continent?
A) South America
B) Alaska
C) Antarctica
D) Africa

Answer: B.
Alaska is not a continent, but it is the 50th state in the United States.

05

What do you call a place in which two streams meet to form a larger stream?
A) Confluence
B) Waterfall
C) Bank
D) Mouth

Answer: A.
When two rivers flow together and join to form one larger river, it is called confluence.

06

What river flows through the rainforests of Brazil?
A) Watusi
B) Kookaburra
C) Amazon
D) Rio Grande

Answer: C.
The Amazon is regarded as the largest river in volume, and it is believed to be the largest river in the world.

07

What do you call a piece of land that is surrounded by water on three sides?
A) Alluvia
B) Triangle
C) Peninsula
D) Island

Answer: C.
A Peninsula is a landmass surrounded by water on three sides. Two countries that are peninsulas are Spain and Portugal.

08

On what continent would you find the Andes Mountains?
A) South America
B) North America
C) Africa
D) Asia

Answer: A.
The Andes Mountains span the entire west coast of South America.

09

Which is the tallest waterfall in the world?
A) Angel Falls
B) Victoria Falls
C) Yosemite Falls
D) Niagara Falls

Answer: A.
The Angel Falls in Venezuela is the highest, uninterrupted waterfall.

10

Which is the largest country in the world?
A) The United States
B) England
C) Turkey
D) Russia

Answer: D.
Russia is the largest country in the world.

11

Which large river flows through London?
A) The Ganges River
B) The Nile
C) The Thames
D) The Great River

Answer: C.
The Thames is a large river in London that runs 215 miles.

12

In which country would you find the Great Pyramid of Giza?
A) India
B) Egypt
C) Japan
D) China

Answer: B.
The Great Pyramid of Giza is one of three giant pyramid-shaped structures outside of Cairo, Egypt that house the dead of the Egyptians. The Great Pyramid of Giza is one of the seven man-made wonders of the world.

13

What two countries border the United States?
A) Canada and Mexico
B) Alaska and Greenland
C) America and Brazil
D) Australia and Africa

Answer: A.
Canada is a country that borders the north of the United States and Mexico borders the south of the United States.

14

Which country has the largest population in the world?
A) Japan
B) America
C) China
D) Africa

Answer: C.
China has a population of almost 1.393 billion people, the largest population in the world.

15

Which city is famous for its canals?
A) Melbourne
B) Venice
C) Delhi
D) Rio de Janeiro

Answer: B.
Venice has many canals, including the Grand Canal, which forms one of the major water-traffic corridors in the city.

16

In what country would you find the Eiffel Tower?
A) Italy
B) France
C) China
D) Nigeria

Answer: B.
The Eiffel Tower was built in France in 1889 to celebrate the French Revolution.

17

In which city is the Golden Gate Bridge located?
A) New Jersey
B) New York
C) California
D) San Francisco

Answer: D.
The Golden Gate Bridge is located in the city of San Francisco.

18

What is the capital of Thailand?
A) Shanghai
B) Bangkok
C) Kolkata
D) Cairo

Answer: B.
Bangkok is a large city in Thailand, and it is the capital of the country.

19

Cairo is the capital of which country?
A) Thailand
B) Indonesia
C) Egypt
D) China

Answer: C.
Cairo is the largest city in Egypt, and it is the capital of the country.

20

What is the capital of England?
A) London
B) Ottawa
C) Pretoria
D) Cairo

Answer: A.
London is a large city in England, and it is the capital of the country.

21

What is the capital city of Canada?
A) Toronto
B) Indianapolis
C) New York City
D) Ottawa

Answer: D.
Ottawa is derived from a word meaning "to trade."

22

What is the capital city of Spain?
A) Buenos Aires
B) Rio de Janeiro
C) Madrid
D) Pretoria

Answer: C.
Madrid is a large culturally significant city, and it is also the capital of Spain.

23

Madagascar is surrounded by which ocean?
A) Atlantic Ocean
B) Pacific Ocean
C) Indian Ocean
D) Mediterranean Sea

Answer: C.
The Indian Ocean is a warm, tropical ocean that surrounds the island of Madagascar.

24

In which mountain range does Mt. Everest lie?
A) Kilimanjaro
B) The Himalayas
C) The Mount Everest Mountain Range
D) Asian Mountain Range

Answer: B.
Mount Everest lies in the mountain range of The Himalayas.

25

How many states are in the United States of America?
A) 50
B) 25
C) 30
D) 55

Answer: A.
There are 50 states in the United States of America.

26

What do the letters "D" and "C" stand for in Washington D.C.?
A) District of California
B) District of Canada
C) District of Columbia
D) District of Calcutta

Answer: C.
The "D" and "C" in Washington D.C. stands for the District of Columbia.

27

On what island is the Statue of Liberty located?
A) Madagascar
B) Statue Island
C) Venice
D) Liberty Island

Answer: D.
The Statue of Liberty is located on Liberty Island in New York City.

28

Europe and Asia are separated by which sea?
A) Indian Ocean
B) Pacific Ocean
C) Mediterranean
D) Atlantic Ocean

Answer: C.
The Mediterranean Sea separates Europe from Asia.

29

Which is the hottest continent on Earth?
A) Europe
B) Asia
C) Africa
D) North America

Answer: C.
Africa is the hottest continent on Earth due to its placement near the Equator.

30

What is the nickname for New York City?
A) The Busy City
B) The Windy City
C) The Big City
D) The Big Apple

Answer: D.
New York is called the Big Apple because of the "big apple" prizes given at racing courses in and around New York.

31

Which Scottish loch or lake is suspected to have a monster?
A) Nessie Lake
B) Loch Ness
C) The Thames
D) The Nile River

Answer: B.
The Loch Ness is a Scottish loch (lake) that is suspected to have the Loch Ness Monster.

32

Which U.S. state used to be called "Deseret?"
A) New York
B) California
C) Nevada
D) Utah

Answer: D.
Utah was previously known as "Deseret."

33

Where are the holy cities of Mecca and Medina located?
A) Iraq
B) Pakistan
C) Saudi Arabia
D) India

Answer: C.
The holy cities of Mecca and Medina are located in Saudi Arabia.

34

Which city is situated on two continents?
A) Istanbul
B) Moscow
C) Rio de Janeiro
D) Rome

Answer: A.
Istanbul is the only city in the world that's spread over two continents, with the Bosphorus Strait forming the dividing line between Europe and Asia.

35

Which continent is the most populous?
A) Europe
B) North America
C) Africa
D) Asia

Answer: D.
60% of the world's population live on the Asian continent.

36

Which is the longest river in Africa?
A) Congo River
B) The Nile
C) Zambezi River
D) Niger

Answer: B.
The Nile is the longest river in Africa. It is 6650 km/4130miles long. The Nile's drainage basin covers 11 countries.

37

Which is the largest capital city in the world (by population)?
A) Tokyo
B) Paris
C) Brasilia
D) New Delhi

Answer: A.
Tokyo is the most populated city in the world. More than 38 million people live in the metropolitan area of Japan's capital city.

38

In which country will you find the city of Naples?
A) Spain
B) Italy
C) Portugal
D) France

Answer: B.
Naples is a city in southern Italy. Nearby is Mount Vesuvius, the still-active volcano that destroyed the nearby Roman town Pompeii.

01

In what year was the World Cup won by England?
A) 1966
B) 1970
C) 1974
D) 1990

Answer: A.
England won the World Cup in 1966.

02

What is the name of the ice hockey team that plays at New York's Madison Square Garden?
A) New York Islanders
B) New York Americans
C) New York Golden Blades
D) New York Rangers

Answer: D.
The New York Rangers play at New York's Madison Square Garden.

03

Which English city has teams called United and Wednesday?
A) Newcastle
B) Birmingham
C) Sheffield
D) Watford

Answer: C.
The English city Sheffield has teams called United and Wednesday.

04

In a professional game, how many clubs can a golfer carry?

A) 10
B) 14
C) 15
D) 18

Answer: B.
A golfer is allowed to carry 14 golf clubs in a professional game.

05

From which country is England's cricket captain Eoin Morgan from?

A) Scotland
B) England
C) Ireland
D) Wales

Answer: C.
England's cricket captain Eoin Morgan is from Ireland.

06

Which city and country will host the 2024 Olympics?

A) Tokyo, Japan
B) Copenhagen, Denmark
C) Los Angeles, United States
D) Paris, France

Answer: A.
The 2024 Olympics will be hosted in Paris, France.

07

What follows a deuce in a game of tennis?
A) Love
B) Advantage
C) Zero
D) Game Point

Answer: B.
A deuce in tennis is followed by an advantage.

08

What basketball team does LeBron James play for?
A) Los Angeles Clippers
B) San Antonio Spurs
C) Los Angeles Lakers
D) Chicago Bulls

Answer: C.
LeBron James plays basketball for the Los Angeles Lakers.

09

In what year did the tennis player Andy Murray win a gold medal in the Olympics?
A) 2008
B) 2012
C) 2020
D) He won a silver medal

Answer: B.
Andy Murray won an Olympic gold medal for tennis in 2012.

10

In Formula One, what does a checkered flag mean?
A) Someone's car has broken down
B) The race has started
C) The session has ended
D) Everyone has been disqualified

Answer: C.
A checkered flag means the session has ended in Formula One.

11

Which golfer has the same first name as a big cat?
A) Tiger Woods
B) Lion Woods
C) Jaguar Woods
D) Cheetah Woods

Answer: A.
Tiger Woods is an American golfer with the same first name as a big cat.

12

What country does the soccer player Lionel Messi play for?
A) Brazil
B) England
C) Argentina
D) Ireland

Answer: C.
Lionel Messi plays for Argentina's soccer team.

13

Which sport is Mo Farah a champion for?
A) Athletics   C) Swimming
B) Football   D) Tennis

Answer: A.
Mo Farah is a famous athletics champion.

14

A caddy is a person that carries the player's bag in which sport?
A) Tennis   C) Soccer
B) Golf   D) Cricket

Answer: B.
A caddy is the person that carries the player's bag in golf.

15

If a player has a hat trick, how many goals are scored?
A) One   C) Three
B) Two   D) Four

Answer: C.
A hat trick is when one player scores three goals in the same game.

16

What swimming stroke has the same name as a flying insect?

A) The butterfly
B) The moth
C) The fly
D) The bumblebee

Answer: A.
The butterfly is a swimming stroke named after a flying insect.

17

In hockey, what is the name of the hard, rubber disc that players hit?

A) Ball
B) Disc
C) Round
D) Puck

Answer: D.
The hard, rubber disc players hit in hockey is called a puck.

18

How many rings are there on the Olympic flag?

A) Seven
B) Five
C) Six
D) 12

Answer: B.
There are five interlinked rings on the Olympic flag

19

In the Harry Potter series, what wizarding sport is played on broomsticks?

A) Quaffle
B) Bludger
C) Broomstick Soccer
D) Quidditch

Answer: D.
Quidditch is a fictional sport played on flying broomsticks in the Harry Potter series.

20

How many vertical stumps make up a cricket wicket?

A) Three
B) Four
C) Five
D) Six

Answer: A.
Three vertical stumps make up a wicket in cricket.

21

Michael Phelps competed in which sport?

A) Tennis
B) Sprinting
C) Track
D) Swimming

Answer: D.
Michael Phelps has won the most Olympic medals in the history of the competition in swimming.

22

In the Olympic athletics, what spear-shaped object is thrown?
A) Spear
B) Javelin
C) Pole
D) Sword

Answer: B.
The spear-shaped object thrown at the Olympics in athletics is called a javelin.

23

Andy Murray is a champion in which sport?
A) Formula One
B) Swimming
C) Gold
D) Tennis

Answer: D.
Andy Murray is an Olympic-winning tennis player.

24

In which country did the Olympic Games originate?
A) Spain
B) India
C) Greece
D) Rome

Answer: C.
The Olympic Games originated in the country of Greece.

25

In badminton, what do players hit?
A) Puck
B) Ball
C) Disc
D) Shuttlecock

Answer: D.
In the game of badminton, a shuttlecock is hit.

26

What is pulled by the teams in a game of tug-of-war?
A) Cloth
B) Fishing line
C) Rope
D) Ice pack

Answer: C.
Tug-of-war is played when two groups of players pull on a rope as hard as they can.

27

Which color jersey does the leader in the Tour de France cycle race wear?
A) Yellow
B) Green
C) Blue
D) Red

Answer: A.
The leader in the Tour de France cycle race wears a yellow jersey.

28
In which sport might you hear the score announced as "30–love?"
A) Tennis C) Rugby
B) Golf D) Football

Answer: A.
In tennis, "love" means zero points.

29
Which American boxer was known as "The Greatest?"
A) Baby Jakes C) Bob Baker
B) Muhammad Ali D) Jason O'Dell

Answer: B.
Muhammad Ali is referred to as "The Greatest" as his boxing was unparalleled.

30
Which sport is also known as ping pong?
A) Table Tennis C) Tennis
B) Badminton D) Rugby

Answer: A.
Table Tennis often called ping pong.

31

Which country has won the soccer world cup the most times?
A) Argentina
B) England
C) United States
D) Brazil

Answer: D.
Brazil has won the soccer world cup five times.

32

How many players are there on a basketball side?
A) Five
B) Six
C) Seven
D) Eight

Answer: A.
Basketball is played with two teams, with five players from each team on the court at one time.

33

Soccer, rugby, cricket, boxing, and golf were all invented in which country?
A) Argentina
B) United Kingdom
C) United States
D) China

Answer: B.
Soccer, rugby, cricket, boxing, and golf were all invented in the United Kingdom.

01

Which of the following devices was invented by Alexander Graham Bell?

A) Telephone
B) Airplane
C) Car
D) Computer

Answer: A.
Alexander Graham Bell invented the telephone. He is also credited as having invented many other things such as the metal detector in 1881.

02

Martin Luther King said, "I have a…"

A) Friend
B) Dream
C) Home
D) Country

Answer: B.
Martin Luther King received a Nobel Peace Prize for his fight against racial inequality in 1964. "I Have a Dream" is his famous speech from 1963.

03

In what century did Queen Victoria rule the British Empire?

A) 20th
B) 17th
C) 19th
D) 18th

Answer: C.
Queen Victoria ruled the United Kingdom from 1837-1901.

04

Which of the following famous politicians drafted the Declaration of Independence?
A) George Bush
B) Bill Clinton
C) Franklin D. Roosevelt
D) Thomas Jefferson

Answer: D.
The Declaration of Independence was published in July of 1776 and was written by Thomas Jefferson.

05

The Mayan Civilization was located in which modern-day country?
A) Brazil
B) Peru
C) Russia
D) Mexico

Answer: D.
The Mayan people of Mexico were known for architecture, art, the calendar, and astrology.

06

Where was the Titanic headed when it hit an iceberg and sank?
A) New York
B) Australia
C) Moscow
D) Paris

Answer: A.
The Titanic sank on the 15th of April 1912, in the North Atlantic Ocean, on its way to New York City.

07

Which English king was famous for having six wives?
A) Edward VIII
B) Richard VIII
C) Richard the Lionheart
D) Henry VIII

Answer: D.
Henry's six wives were named Catherine of Aragon, Anne Boleyn, Jane Seymour, Anne of Cleves, Kathryn Howard, and Catherine Parr.

08

Which of these cities was divided by a wall from 1961 to 1989?
A) Washington D.C.
B) Berlin
C) London
D) Rome

Answer: B.
A wall divided East and West Berlin from 1961 to 1989.

09

Which of the following ships was one of Christopher Columbus's famous ships?
A) Santa Mary
B) Pinta
C) Titanic
D) Dina

Answer: B.
Columbus sailed from Spain with three ships: The Nina, the Pinta, and the Santa Maria.

10

Leif Eriksson was the son of which famous Viking?
A) Rolo the White
B) Dan the Blue
C) Erik the Red
D) Simon the Yellow

Answer: C.
Erik the Red was Leif Eriksson's father and is considered the first Viking to sail to North America.

11

Who invented the lightbulb?
A) J.P. Morgan
B) Henry Ford
C) Thomas Edison
D) Alexander Graham Bell

Answer: C.
Thomas Edison also invented the phonograph and the motion picture camera.

12

Who was the first president of the United States?
A) George Washington
B) Abraham Lincoln
C) Thomas Jefferson
D) Andrew Jackson

Answer: A.
George Washington served as the first president of the United States from 1789 to 1797.

13

Which Pope reigned the earliest?
A) Clement XIV
B) Pius X
C) Innocent XIII
D) Leo XIII

Answer: C.
Pope Innocent XIII began his reign in May 1721 and ended in March 1724.

14

Attila, the ruler of the Huns, battled which empire?
A) Chinese   C) Romans
B) Egyptians   D) Greeks

Answer: C.
Attila the Hun was one of the most feared enemies of the Roman Empire.

15

Edward Jenner, an English Physician, invented the vaccination for which disease?
A) Mumps   C) Polio
B) Measles   D) Smallpox

Answer: D.
The vaccination for smallpox, invented by Edward Jenner, was the world's first vaccine.

16

Florence Nightingale became famous during which conflict?
A) Falklands War   C) Crimean War
B) World War I   D) World War II

Answer: C.
During the Crimean War, Florence was known as "The Lady with the Lamp."

17

Henry VII was a member of which royal house?
A) Stuart   C) Tudor
B) Windsor   D) Hanover

Answer: C.
Henry VII was the first monarch of the House of Tudor.

18

Henry McCarty was the real name of which American Old West gunfighter?
A) Billy the Kid
B) Kid Curry
C) Wild Bill
D) Butch Cassidy

Answer: A.
Billy the Kid's real name was Henry McCarty, and he was also known as William H. Bonney.

19

When was the first Nobel Prize awarded?
A) 1901
B) 1922
C) 1880
D) 1911

Answer: A.
The Nobel Prizes originated from a will left by a Swedish chemist named Alfred Nobel, and the first prize was awarded on December 10, 1901.

20

Which of these historic events happened before the others?
A) Treaty of Tordesillas
B) War of the Roses Begins
C) Battle of Bosworth
D) Hundred Years War Ends

Answer: D.
The Hundred Years War ended in 1453.

21

On which city was the first atomic bomb attack?
A) Beijing
B) Tokyo
C) Hiroshima
D) Beirut

Answer: C.
Hiroshima, a modern city on Japan's Honshu Island, was largely destroyed by an atomic bomb during World War II.

22

Which former Beatle organized a concert to raise funds for refugees fleeing the Bangladesh Genocide in 1971?
A) Ringo Starr
B) John Lennon
C) George Harrison
D) Paul McCartney

Answer: C.
The Concert for Bangladesh was organized by George Harrison and took place in Madison Square Garden in New York City.

23

In what previous occupation did the painter, Alan LaVern Bean become famous?
A) Actor
B) Writer
C) Politician
D) Astronaut

Answer: D.
Alan LaVern Bean was the fourth person to walk on the moon.

24

Which singer made his debut in the film Love Me Tender in 1956?
A) Bobby Darin
B) Ricky Nelson
C) Elvis Presley
D) Frank Sinatra

Answer: C.
Love Me Tender by Elvis Presley was set in Texas after the American Civil War.

25

How is Joan of Arc, the heroine of France, also known?
A) The Maid of Orleans
B) The Servant of Orleans
C) The Savior of Orleans
D) The Mother of Orleans

Answer: A.
Joan of Arc, also known as The Maid of Orleans, was burned at the stake on the 30th of May 1434 for heresy.

26

In what year did the infamous "Jack the Ripper'" commit his crimes?
A) 1906
B) 1854
C) 1924
D) 1888

Answer: D.
Jack the Ripper is a nameless serial killer that committed his murders in 1888 in the Whitechapel district of London.

27 Mohammed Morsi was sentenced to 20 years in prison in which nation in 2015?
A) France
B) Spain
C) Turkey
D) Egypt

Answer: D.
Morsi was the fifth president of Egypt.

28 Who built the Taj Mahal in India?
A) Jahangir
B) Shah Alam
C) Sher Shah Suri
D) Shah Jahan

Answer: D.
The Taj Mahal is a mausoleum inspired by Shah Jahan's love for his wife.

29 Married in 1582, who was Anne Hathaway's husband?
A) Francis Drake
B) Sir Francis Bacon
C) William Shakespeare
D) Henry the Eighth

Answer: C.
Anne was married to Shakespeare until her death in 1663 at the age of 67 years.

30 Which U.S. President used the slogan "The Buck Stops Here?"
A) Nixon
B) Kennedy
C) Regan
D) Truman

Answer: D.
President Truman had a sign with this slogan on his desk.

31

Which archaeologist discovered the tomb of Tutankhamen?
A) Pierre Montet
B) Alexander Thom
C) Howard Carter
D) Alfred Kidder

Answer: C.
Tutankhamen was a young Pharaoh of Egypt. His crypt was discovered in 1922 by Howard Carter, and it is still being explored to this day.

32

In which city was the world's first underground railway open?
A) San Francisco, United States
B) Beijing, China
C) London, England
D) Paris, France

Answer: C.
The London Underground is the oldest metro system in the world, with services operating from 1890.

33

What continent did Dr. Livingstone explore?
A) Africa
B) Asia
C) Australia
D) Antarctica

Answer: A.
David Livingstone was a Scottish missionary, abolitionist, and physician known for his explorations of Africa. He crossed the continent during the mid-19th century.

34

When did Great Britain get the atomic bomb?
A) 1867
C) 1952
B) 1974
D) 1914

Answer: C.
Britain was the 3rd country to get the atomic bomb.

35

In Greek Mythology, what did Prometheus steal from the gods to give to man?
A) Water
C) Love
B) Fire
D) Hope

Answer: B.
Prometheus stole fire from the gods and gave it to mankind.

36

The Taj Mahal, the ivory-white marble mausoleum, was built in what century?
A) 18th
C) 16th
B) 19th
D) 17th

Answer: D.
The Taj Mahal was completed in 1653.

37

Which country first used paper money?
A) Japan
C) Mongolia
B) India
D) China

Answer: D.
Paper money was invented in China in the century.

CHAPTER 6
FOOD

01

A popular meal in Central Europe, "goulash," originated in what country?
A) Hungary
B) France
C) Italy
D) Spain

Answer: A.
The main ingredients in goulash are meat, noodles, vegetables, spices, and paprika.

02

The rice dish "paella" comes from which country?
A) Argentina
B) Brazil
C) Africa
D) Spain

Answer: D.
Paella is a Spanish dish prepared with an array of seafood and flavorful rice.

03

Deer meat is known by what name?
A) Pork
B) Venison
C) Chicken
D) Beef

Answer: B.
Venison is the word given for deer meat.

04

"Limburger" is a famous cheese from which nation?
A) Spain
B) Belgium
C) Italy
D) France

Answer: B.
Limburger is known for its strong smell.

05

What food is used as the base of guacamole?
A) Chickpeas
B) Avocado
C) Melon
D) Cucumber

Answer: B.
Guacamole is a Mexican dip that is made of avocado.

06

The Pizza Hut franchise began in what country?
A) Africa
B) India
C) Australia
D) United States

Answer: D.
Pizza Hut began in the United States and now has 18,000 restaurants in over 100 countries.

07

What is the sweet substance made by bees?
A) Nectar
B) Pollen
C) Honey
D) Sugar

Answer: C.
Honey is a sweet, sticky substance created by bees.

08

India is the largest producer of which fruit?
A) Apples
B) Spices
C) Oranges
D) Bananas

Answer: D.
Indian food is often eaten off banana leaves in India.

09

Lures, reels, rods, hooks, baits, and nets are common equipment used in what food gathering method?
A) Hunting
B) Gathering
C) Fishing
D) Collecting

Answer: C.
In some countries, fishing is the primary method of finding food.

10

The range of vegetables, fruits, meats, nuts, grains, herbs, and spices used in cooking are known as what?
A) Herbs
B) Spices
C) Ingredients
D) Measurements

Answer: C.
Ingredients are the raw materials added to the food while cooking.

11

Foods rich in starch such as pasta and bread are often known by what word starting with the letter C?
A) Calzone
B) Carbohydrates
C) Candy
D) Cold-meat

Answer: B.
Carbohydrates, such as spaghetti and bread, are the body's primary source of energy.

12 What is the popular food used to carve jack-o-lanterns during Halloween?
A) Butternut
C) Watermelons
B) Pumpkins
D) Pineapple

Answer: B.
The act of carving jack-o-lanterns out of pumpkins during Halloween is an age-old tradition in the United States and Canada.

13 Fruit preserves made from citrus fruits, sugar, and water are known as what?
A) Jam
C) Marmalade
B) Jelly
D) None of the above

Answer: C.
Marmalade is any jam preserve made from citrus fruit, such as oranges and lemons.

14 Dairy products are generally made from what common liquid?
A) Milk
C) Yogurt
B) Lactose
D) Cheese

Answer: A.
Milk is the basic foundation of dairy products, and it is high in lactose.

15

In what climates do coconut trees grow best?
A) Cool
B) Hot
C) Warm
D) Rainy

Answer: C.
Coconuts are known to grow in tropical climates such as South America and Africa.

16

What is another name for maize?
A) Corn
B) Meal
C) Stalks
D) Sweetcorn

Answer: A.
Corn is a staple food in many countries, and it provides many healthy vitamins and minerals.

17

Chiffon, marble, and Bundt are types of what?
A) Candy
B) Bread
C) Cheese
D) Cake

Answer: D.
Cakes are common treats at birthday parties and weddings.

18

Steak tartare is a dish that is...?
A) Dried beef
B) Heavily salted beef
C) Heavily peppered beef
D) Uncooked beef

Answer: D.
Steak tartare originated in France in the early 20th century.

19

In Mexican cuisine, which of these foods is a soft, finely-ground wheat flour flatbread?
A) Burrito
B) Taco
C) Sapote
D) Tortilla

Answer: D.
Tortillas are used to make burritos and tacos, as well as other Mexican dishes.

20

What kind of food is a "pumpernickel?"
A) Pasta
B) Rice
C) Bread
D) Wine

Answer: C.
The pumpernickel originated in Westphalia in Germany in the 1400s.

21

What is the main ingredient in the traditional Russian dish "coulibiac?"
A) Fish
B) Chicken
C) Beef
D) Pork

Answer: A.
A coulibiac is a dish made from fish, mushrooms, eggs, onions, and spices.

22

Sushi is the national dish of which country?
A) Japan
B) South Africa
C) Ukraine
D) Portugal

Answer: A.
Japanese curries and ramen are also considered the national dishes of Japan.

23

What is the natural human diet?
A) Omnivores
B) Carnivores
C) Herbivores
D) None of the above

Answer: A.
Human beings are able to digest and eat fruits, vegetables, and meat.

24

What is the name of the hot green paste often served in Japanese restaurants?
A) Stigabi
B) Wasabi
C) Montabi
D) Lumbadi

Answer: B.
Wasabi is also known as Japanese horseradish.

25

Which geographical feature is also the name of a type of lettuce?
A) Sea
B) Mountain
C) Iceberg
D) Volcano

Answer: C.
Lettuce was first planted and cultivated by the ancient Egyptians.

26

Native to South Asia, the kumquat is a small variety of which fruit?
A) Peach
B) Orange
C) Apple
D) Pear

Answer: B.
Kumquats are the only citrus fruit that can be eaten with the skin.

27

The famous bird's nest soup, containing the saliva of a swiftlet, is a dish native to which country?
A) South Africa
B) India
C) China
D) Russia

Answer: C.
The bird's nest soup is known for its great flavor and nutritional value.

28

Which of these is not a common variety of asparagus?
A) White
B) Red
C) Purple
D) Green

Answer: B.
Red. 93% of the asparagus composition is water.

29

In Indian cuisine, what is "roti?"
A) Rice
B) Spiced meat
C) Pasta
D) Bread

Answer: D.
Roti is made from stone ground wholemeal flour and water.

30

The name for which Italian food item comes from the Italian word for "slipper?"
A) Canape
B) Ciabatta
C) Ceviche
D) Cannelloni

Answer: B.
Ciabatta is a white bread made with flour and olive oil.

31

In terms of food, a "flageolet" is what?
A) Vegetable
B) Bean
C) Fruit
D) Nut

Answer: B.
A flageolet is a small, green bean shaped like a kidney.

32

Which Middle Eastern food is a light paste made from toasted sesame seeds?
A) Tahini
B) Ghee
C) Basmati
D) Phyllo

Answer: A.
Tahini is water-soaked and crushed sesame seeds that form a paste.

33

What country produces the most potatoes?
A) China
B) United States
C) Ireland
D) Russia

Answer: A.
China is now the world's top potato producer, followed by India, Russia, and Ukraine. The United States is the 5th largest producer of potatoes in the world.

34

Oolong, Darjeeling, and Rooibos are all types of what?
A) Tea
B) Pasta
C) Coffee
D) Bread

Answer: A.
Other than water, tea is the most common beverage in the world.

35

Raisins are the dried version of which fruit?
A) Cherry
B) Apricot
C) Grape
D) Peach

Answer: C.
Raisins are often eaten with nuts, to enhance their flavor.

36

Marzipan is made with what kind of nut?
A) Almond
B) Cashew
C) Pecan
D) Walnut

Answer: A.
Marzipan is most commonly used as a filling for marzipan cookies, for coloring and shaping into fun designs, or for covering cakes like fruit cake. It is similar to almond paste but contains more sugar so it's sweeter.

37

Which vitamin helps our body to fight colds and other illnesses?
A) Vitamin A
B) Vitamin B
C) Vitamin C
D) Vitamin D

Answer: C.
Vitamin C is often thought of as a natural cold remedy. The nutrient is featured in supplements promising to boost the immune system.

CHAPTER 7
NATURE

01

A lobster's teeth are located in which part of its body?
A) Stomach
B) Mouth
C) Legs
D) Claws

Answer: A.
The lobster has teeth in its stomach and has ten walking legs.

02

How many hearts does an octopus have?
A) Zero
B) One
C) Two
D) Three

Answer: D.
There are about 300 different species of octopi.

03

"Apiology" is the scientific study of what?
A) Honey bees
B) Earthquakes
C) Trout
D) Mars

Answer: A.
There are seven species of the honey bee.

04

Pneumonia affects which part of the human body?

A) Kidneys
B) Lungs
C) Heart
D) Gums

Answer: B.
Pneumonia affects 450 million people every year.

05

Brass is a metallic alloy that is made from copper and what other chemical element?

A) Carbon
B) Zinc
C) Lead
D) Iron

Answer: B.
An alloy is a mixture of two metallic elements.

06

Which of these animals is an herbivore?

A) Cow
B) Shark
C) Dog
D) Eagle

Answer: A.
An herbivore is an animal that only eats plants.

07

Which of these is another word/phrase for tsunami?
A) Tidal wave
B) Hurricane
C) Tornado
D) Earthquake

Answer: A.
Tsunamis are often caused by earthquakes on the seabed.

08

What do you call a person who studies rocks?
A) Geologist
B) Biologist
C) Archaeologist
D) Ornithologist

Answer: A.
Geologists are often employed by oil and mining companies.

09

Gregor Mendel performed experiments on which of the following?
A) Dogs
B) Monkeys
C) Plants
D) Trees

Answer: C.
Gregor Mendel studied the genes of pea plants.

10 The energy used by most living beings on the earth to feed, move, and reproduce all comes from what original source?
A) Soil
B) Twinkies
C) Water
D) Sun

Answer: D.
The sun provides energy for all living processes.

11 Which of the following lives in a cocoon for part of its life cycle?
A) Lobster
B) Crab
C) Moth
D) Mollusk

Answer: C.
Caterpillars form cocoons before they turn into moths.

12 Which of the following vertebrates lacks a bony spine?
A) Whale
B) Salamander
C) Frog
D) Lamprey

Answer: D.
A lamprey is a long sea organism with many rows of teeth.

13 Why do fish swim in schools?
A) Surround prey
B) Confuse predators
C) Chase away larger fish
D) Find food

Answer: B.
Fish swim in schools to avoid and confuse predators.

14 Rabies is caused by which infectious agent?
A) Virus   C) Fungus
B) Worm   D) Alga

Answer: A.
Rabies is a virus that affects the central nervous system of a mammal.

15 Which famous scientist introduced the idea of natural selection?
A) Ned Stark   C) The Pope
B) Charles Darwin   D) Helen Keller

Answer: B.
Charles Darwin introduced natural selection as a way to explain evolution.

16

A person who studies biology is known as a what?
A) Geologist
B) Scientist
C) Biologist
D) Doctor

Answer: C.
Biologists study the way living organisms survive and thrive.

17

Botany is the study of what?
A) Animals
B) Plants
C) Food
D) Rocks

Answer: B.
Botanists study all living plants.

18

Animals that eat both plants and other animals are known as what?
A) Carnivores
B) Omnivores
C) Herbivores
D) None of the above

Answer: B.
Omnivores are able to eat both plant and animal matter.

19 Bacterial infections in humans can be treated with what?
A) Vaccines
C) Pills
B) Medication
D) Antibiotics

Answer: D.
The first antibiotic ever discovered was penicillin.

20 A single piece of coiled DNA is known as a?
A) Gene
C) Coil
B) Chromosome
D) Spring

Answer: B.
The human body has 46 chromosomes.

21 A group of dog offspring is known as a what?
A) Pack
C) Team
B) Group
D) Litter

Answer: D.
A group of puppies is known as a litter.

22

What is the area of biology that is devoted to the study of fungi?
A) Biology
B) Microbiology
C) Fungology
D) Mycology

Answer: D.
Mycology is the study of fungi and the ways in which fungi live.

23

What is the process used by plants to convert sunlight into food?
A) Photosynthesis
B) Food Synthesis
C) Food Production
D) Light Conversion

Answer: A.
Photosynthesis is the plant's method of making food out of sunlight.

24

The death of every member of a particular species is known as what?
A) Memorial
B) Extinction
C) Endangerment
D) Death

Answer: B.
Many endangered creatures are in danger of becoming extinct.

25

The process of pasteurization is named after which famous French microbiologist?

A) Larry Pasteur
B) Louis Pasteur
C) Luke Pasteur
D) Louis Paster

Answer: B.
Louis Pasteur developed the system of pasteurizing milk to purify it.

26

A change of the DNA in an organism that results in a new trait is known as a what?

A) Development
B) Growth
C) Evolution
D) Mutation

Answer: D.
Mutation is any change in the DNA of an organism.

27

What is the name of the layer of the earth's atmosphere that absorbs the majority of the potentially damaging ultraviolet light from the sun?

A) Protection Layer
B) Ozone Layer
C) Ultraviolet Protection Layer
D) Ultraviolet Layer

Answer: B.
The Ozone Layer is being destroyed due to pollution.

28 What is the second most common gas found in the air we breathe?
A) Nitrogen
B) Methane
C) Carbon Dioxide
D) Oxygen

Answer: D.
Oxygen makes up 21% of the air we breathe.

29 The gemstone ruby is typically what color?
A) Blue
B) Green
C) Yellow
D) Red

Answer: D.
Rubies are the birthstones for the month of July.

30 Balls or irregular lumps of ice that fall from clouds (often during thunderstorms) are known as what?
A) Drizzle
B) Shower
C) Hail
D) Rain

Answer: C.
Hail is rain droplets that have frozen due to cold weather.

31

Stratus, cirrus, cumulus, and nimbus are types of what?
A) Clouds
B) Trees
C) Fish
D) Birds

Answer: A.
There are many different types of clouds with unique shapes and colors depending on the rain.

32

A thermometer is a device used to measure what?
A) Temperature
B) Weight
C) Height
D) Color

Answer: A.
A thermometer is used to detect the temperature of any object.

33

What is the name of a scientist who studies weather?
A) Botanist
B) Biologist
C) Climatologist
D) Meteorologist

Answer: D.
Meteorologists use special tools to study and predict the weather.

34

The mass of the earth is made up mostly of which two elements?
A) Iron and Oxygen
B) Carbon and Oxygen
C) Zinc and Carbon
D) Iron and Carbon

Answer: A.
Iron makes 32% of the mass of the earth, and oxygen makes up 30% of the mass of the earth.

35

What existing bird has the largest wingspan?
A) Stork
B) Swan
C) Condor
D) Albatross

Answer: D.
The wandering albatross has a wingspan that ranges from eight to 11.5 feet.

36

Fill in the blank: Out of these pets, there are the most pet ..... in the United States.
A) Birds
B) Cats
C) Dogs
D) Horses

Answer: B.
A 2017–2018 survey from the American Pet Products Association found that there were about 94.2 million pet cats in the United States compared to 89.7 million pet dogs. There were also 20.3 million pet birds and 7.6 million pet horses.

37

What are female elephants called?
A) Mares
B) Sows
C) Cows
D) Dams

Answer: C.
Female elephants are called cows. Males are called bulls. And the babies are called calves.

38

Which of the following animals sleeps standing up?
A) Gorillas
B) Flamingos
C) Hedgehogs
D) Ravens

Answer: B.
Flamingos sleep standing up because the salt flats they live on are too salty and stinging for them to sit down.

01

Where is the "Polar Express" going?
A) San Francisco
B) Australia
C) The North Pole
D) The East Coast

Answer: C.
The "Polar Express" is travelling to see Santa in The North Pole.

02

From what film did "Spider-Pig" become the shortest song to reach the British Top 40?
A) Family Guy
B) The Simpsons Movie
C) Charlotte's Web
D) The Lorax

Answer: B.
Homer Simpson sings the song to a pig he has rescued.

03

In The Chronicles of Narnia, what animal is Aslan?
A) Bird
B) Cheetah
C) Lion
D) Tiger

Answer: C.
Aslan is said to represent God in The Chronicles of Narnia.

04

Manny, Sid, and Diego are trapped in what in "Ice Age: Continental Drift?"
A) Iceberg
B) Piece of ice
C) Boat
D) Tree trunk

Answer: B.
A slab of ice breaks off during the continental drift in the movie.

05

In The Lorax, what color is the Lorax?
A) Purple
B) Green
C) Orange
D) Blue

Answer: C.
The Lorax is the guardian of the trees.

06

What superpower does Violet have in the movie The Incredibles?
A) Super strength
B) Invisibility
C) Telekinesis
D) Fire

Answer: B.
Violet can turn invisible and create force-fields to protect herself and her family.

07

Which chipmunk from Alvin and the Chipmunks has nightmares and gets into bed with Dave?
A) Theo
B) Theodore
C) Tyron
D) Thomas

Answer: B.
The other two chipmunks are named Simon and Alvin.

08

What is the name of Mulan's horse?
A) Altivo
B) Ling Ling
C) Mooshu
D) Khan

Answer: D.
Khan is a black and white stallion.

09

In the movie Monsters, Inc., who is big and tall with blue fur and purple spots?
A) Mike
B) Boo
C) Sully
D) Randell

Answer: C.
Sully scares children and collects screams to power The Monster City.

10

Who are Ella's stepsisters in the film Ella Enchanted?
A) Anastasia and Drizelda
B) Sam and Kat
C) Hattie and Olive
D) Lara and Lane

Answer: C.
The two evil stepsisters are Hattie and Olive.

11

In The Chronicles of Narnia, what is the first thing Lucy sees when she enters the forest?
A) Beaver
B) Lion
C) Witch
D) Lamppost

Answer: D.
Lucy is the youngest of the four Pevensie children.

12

What is the name of Woody's horse in Toy Story 2?
A) Mr. Pickles
B) Lightning
C) Bullseye
D) Lane

Answer: C.
Bullseye is a brown horse.

13

In Happy Feet, who is the penguin who can't sing?
A) Mumble
B) Gloria
C) Zepp
D) Luna

Answer: A.
Mumble is a tap-dancing penguin that can't sing.

14

In Madagascar, what animal was Marty?
A) Lion
B) Hippo
C) Zebra
D) Giraffe.

Answer: C.
Marty is a zebra that longs to visit the wild.

15

Who is Wreck-It Ralph's enemy in Wreck-It Ralph?
A) Fix-It Fred
B) Fix-It Felix, Jr.
C) Fix-It Ted
D) Fix-It Seymour

Answer: B.
Fix-It Felix, Jr. fixes objects as Wreck-It Ralph breaks them.

16

In The Princess Diaries 2: Royal Engagement, what royal position is Princess Mia about to claim?
A) Princess of Wales
B) Princess of France
C) Queen of Genovia
D) Princess of Genovia

Answer: C.
Princess Mia must marry a prince to become Queen of Genovia.

17

What is the name of the dog in the movie Son of the Mask?
A) Spot
B) Spike
C) Fluffy
D) Otis

Answer: D.
Otis turns into an alter-ego when he puts on the mask.

18

What candy was used to lure E.T. in the 1982 movie E.T.: The Extra-Terrestrial?
A) M&Ms
B) Skittles
C) Reese's Pieces
D) Cookies

Answer: C.
The little boy and girl in E.T. use Reese's Pieces to lure E.T. around.

19

What is the name of the Pickles' family dog in Rugrats Go Wild?
A) Fluffy
B) Spike
C) Spot
D) Randy

Answer: B.
Spike is a brown spotted dog that looks after the toddlers.

20

In the movie Monsters, Inc., what does the company Monsters, Inc. do?
A) Makes food
B) Build's skyscrapers
C) Generates electricity
D) Sings lullabies

Answer: C.
The Monster City uses children's screams to power the city.

21

Who are the kids in the movie Spy Kids 3D: Game Over?
A) Sophia and Gomez
B) Carmen and Juni
C) Fred and Alex
D) Laura and Jim

Answer: B.
Juni enters a video game world to save his sister, Carmen.

22

In Bridge to Terabithia, at which sport was Jesse trying to beat the other boys?
A) Football
B) Rugby
C) Cricket
D) Running

Answer: D.
Jesse tries to win, but a girl named Leslie beats him.

23

In Madagascar 3, Dubois gets arrested in which city?

A) Rome
B) Paris
C) New York
D) Venice

Answer: A.

The animals travel around the world performing for a circus.

24

What surrounds the town of Springfield in The Simpsons Movie?

A) Gate
B) Wall
C) Fence
D) Giant dome

Answer: D.

A giant dome surrounds the city, but the Simpsons escape.

25

What animated movie features Flik, Hopper, and Manny?

A) Ants
B) A Bug's Life
C) Tangled
D) Frozen

Answer: B.

Flik is an ant, Hopper is a grasshopper, and Manny is a ladybug.

26

What present does the boy choose in The Polar Express?

A) Toy train
B) Ball
C) Silver bell
D) Cricket bat

Answer: C.
The boy in The Polar Express travels to the North Pole to ask Santa for his gift.

27

When Nemo was put in a fish tank in Finding Nemo, what new name did the other fish give him?

A) Stripes
B) Sharkbait
C) Clown
D) Fishie

Answer: B.
Nemo is given the name Sharkbait when he manages to block the filter in the fish tank for their escape.

28

What kind of animal is Ozzie in Over the Hedge?

A) Tortoise
B) Skunk
C) Opossum
D) Badger

Answer: C.
Ozzie has a daughter, who he is trying to teach to play dead.

29

What is the name of Anne Hathaway's character in The Princess Diaries 2: Royal Engagement?
A) Mia Thermopolis
C) Martha Thermopolis
B) Mia Rhodes
D) Maria Thermopolis

Answer: A.
Mia learns that she is secretly a princess of Genovia.

30

In Ice Age: The Meltdown, what animal is Manny?
A) Human Being
C) Saber-tooth tiger
B) Sloth
D) Mammoth

Answer: D.
A mammoth is a prehistoric elephant species with giant tusks.

31

In the movie Over the Hedge, what does R.J. owe Vincent the Bear?
A) Money
C) Check
B) Food
D) Green ball

Answer: B.
R.J. uses the forest animals to gather food for Vincent the Bear.

32

In The Chronicles of Narnia, who are the four Pevensie children?
A) Lucy, Peter, Susan, Edmund
B) Lara, Pike, Sarah, Edward
C) Cat, Jim, Steven, Phoebe
D) Kate, Jeff, Ann, Laurence

Answer: A.
The four Pevensie children are sons and daughters of Mr. Pevensie and his wife, Helen.

33

Where do the characters in The Lorax live?
A) Knoxville   C) Thneedville
B) Springfield   D) Kneeville

Answer: C.
The town is called Thneedville after the invention of the Thneed.

34

Who captures Nemo at the beginning of Finding Nemo?
A) Dentist   C) Gardener
B) Doctor   D) Fisherman

Answer: A.
The dentist keeps his exotic fish in a fish tank at his dentistry.

35

In the movie Toy Story, to whom does Woody belong?
A) Buzz
C) Sid
B) Andy
D) Billy

Answer: B.
Woody is Andy's favorite toy.

36

In the movie The Little Mermaid, what is Ariel's little fish friend's name?
A) Flounder
C) Chip
B) Sebastian
D) Eric

Answer: A.
Flounder is Ariel's little yellow fish buddy.

37

In the animated movie Madagascar 3, what do Alex and the gang join?
A) A travelling circus
B) A travelling musical show
C) The army
D) The zoo

Answer: A.
The Madagascar animals join a struggling European circus to get back to New York, but they find themselves being pursued by a psychotic animal control officer.

01

In the story of Snow White and the Seven Dwarfs, how did the evil witch poison Snow White?
A) With an apple
B) With a doughnut
C) With a sandwich
D) With a cake

Answer: A.
Snow White falls into a deep sleep after eating the apple.

02

In the fairy tale about the princesses who dance all night, who discovers their secret?
A) Witch
B) Prince
C) Soldier
D) Woodcutter

Answer: C.
The old soldier is given a special cape, which makes him invisible.

03

Which of these fairy tale characters loses a shoe?
A) Red Rose
B) Belle
C) Snow White
D) Cinderella

Answer: D.
Cinderella loses her glass slipper as she is leaving the ball.

04

In the fairy tale version of Bluebeard, what does Bluebeard's wife try to clean?

A) Her shoes
B) A key
C) Bluebeard's robe
D) Bluebeard's bed

Answer: B.
Bluebeard's wife tries to clean the key because it is stained with blood.

05

In which popular story would you find a talking cricket?

A) Cinderella
B) Peter Pan
C) Pinocchio
D) Briar Rose

Answer: C.
The cricket acts as Pinocchio's conscience in the book.

06

In the story of Jack and the Beanstalk, which of these items is not an item that Jack stole from the giant?

A) Sword
B) Goose
C) Harp
D) Bag of gold

Answer: A.
Jack uses an ax to cut down the beanstalk and kill the giant.

07

The character of Maleficent appears in which fairy tale?
A) Red Rose
B) Thumbelina
C) Snow White
D) Sleeping Beauty

Answer: D.
Maleficent is an evil fairy that curses Sleeping Beauty.

08

In the Grimm's German fairy tale, Rapunzel, what was the name of the person who imprisoned Rapunzel?
A) Dame Wanda
B) Dame Gothel
C) Lady Griselda
D) Lady Satin

Answer: B.
Dame Gothel keeps Rapunzel in a tower without a door for her to escape.

09

Which of these is not one of the seven dwarfs?
A) Dopey
B) Happy
C) Dippy
D) Grumpy

Answer: C.
The other four dwarfs are Bashful, Doc, Sneezy, and Sleepy.

10

In the classic version of Cinderella, how many stepsisters does Cinderella have?

A) Zero
B) Two
C) Three
D) Seven

Answer: B.
Cinderella's father marries a woman with two evil daughters.

11

What did the seven dwarfs do for a living?

A) Woodcutters
B) Farmers
C) Hunters
D) Miners

Answer: D.
The seven dwarfs are miners that mine for diamonds.

12

In the tale of Rumpelstiltskin, what does the miller's daughter do?

A) Dance
B) Sing
C) Spins straw into gold
D) Catches the golden goose

Answer: C.
Rumpelstiltskin teaches the miller's daughter how to spin straw into gold.

13

In the story of The Snow Queen by Hans Christian Anderson, where does the Queen live?
A) The Alps
B) The North Pole
C) The Rockies
D) Russia

Answer: A.
The Snow Queen lives in a huge, frozen palace made of ice.

14

Who does Little Red Riding Hood want to visit?
A) Her sister
B) Her grandmother
C) Her aunt
D) The queen

Answer: B.
She stops to pick flowers for her grandmother when she is confronted by a wolf.

15

In the most popular version of the story Beauty and the Beast, what happens to Beauty's sisters?
A) They were forced to work as miners
B) They were turned into statues
C) They were turned into birds
D) They are banished

Answer: B.
Beauty's two sisters are turned into statues at the front of the castle.

16

What kind of creature is Thumbelina expected to marry after she is kidnapped?
A) Frog
B) Wasp
C) Snake
D) Raven

Answer: A.
Thumbelina is rescued from a terrible marriage to a frog.

17

In the fairy tale version of Bluebeard, what is Bluebeard's wife told not to do?
A) Enter a small room
B) Invite friends to the castle
C) Talk to her sister
D) Go into the woods

Answer: A.
Bluebeard forbids his wife from entering a small room in the castle.

18

In the story of The Bremen Town Musicians, which of these animals is not found in the story?
A) Donkey
B) Cat
C) Rooster
D) Owl

Answer: D.
The fourth animal in the story of The Bremen Town Musicians is a dog.

19 In Hans Christians Anderson's story The Snow Queen, what do the Queen's tears turn into?
A) Snowflakes
B) Butterflies
C) Rain
D) Flowers

Answer: D.
The Snow Queen's turn into edelweiss flowers that grow in the Alps.

20 In the original story, Hansel and Gretel get assistance from what kind of creature on their way home from the witch's home?
A) Duck
B) Horse
C) Eagle
D) Frog

Answer: A.
After Hansel and Gretel kill the witch, the duck helps them cross a body of water.

21 In the story of the dancing princesses, how many princesses were there?
A) Seven
B) 12
C) Three
D) Five

Answer: B.
The 12 dancing princesses dance all night, and in the morning, their shoes are worn out.

22

In what year was Sleeping Beauty first published?
A) 1232
B) 1787
C) 1634
D) 1525

Answer: C.
Sleeping Beauty was published by Charles Perrault in 1634.

23

What name does the prince give Thumbelina in the original fairytale?
A) Fiona
B) Maia
C) Jasmine
D) Meredith

Answer: B.
When the prince saw Thumbelina, he decided the name Maia was prettier for her.

24

What did Hansel and Gretel use to leave a trail to find their way back home?
A) Torn paper
B) Gumdrops
C) Leaves
D) Breadcrumbs

Answer: D.
Hansel and Gretel leave a trail of breadcrumbs so they do not get lost.

25

What does the name "Rumpelstiltskin" mean?
A) Wrinkled little man
B) Crazy little man
C) Little name stealer
D) Little rattle stilt

Answer: D.
A little rattle stilt is a type of goblin.

26

What was the color of the apple that the witch gave to Snow White to eat?
A) Red
B) Green
C) White and red
D) Red and yellow

Answer: C.
The Queen cut open the red apple and ate the white, which had no poison.

27

Who published the original Rapunzel fairy tale?
A) Andrew Lang
B) The Grimm Brothers
C) Aesop
D) Aarne Thompson

Answer: B.
Unlike many of the Grimm Fairy Tales, Rapunzel has a happy ending.

28

What lives under the bridge the goats must cross in Three Billy Goats Gruff?
A) Dragon
B) Witch
C) Goblin
D) Troll

Answer: D.
The Three Billy Goats Gruff originated in Norway.

29

What were the names of the Three Little Pigs?
A) Larry, Peter, Paul
B) Oscar, Hamlet, Ribsy
C) Twinkle, Winkle, Wrinkle
D) Not mentioned

Answer: D.
Although there are many adaptations of The Three Little Pigs, they are still nameless.

30

In The Frog Prince, how did the frog turn into a prince?
A) The princess throws him against a wall in disgust
B) The princess pats him on the head
C) The king commanded him to change
D) The princess made a wish

Answer: A.
The princess throws the frog against a wall in disgust and he turns into a prince.

31

In Pinocchio, what does the puppet do to the cricket to get him to stop giving him unwanted advice?
A) Feeds him to a crow
B) Buries him in the garden
C) Traps him in a jar
D) Throws a hammer at him

Answer: D.
The cricket is killed when Pinocchio throws a hammer at it because he longer wants his advice.

32

In the fairytale The Princess on the Glass Hill, what three objects does the princess hold?
A) A sword, a crown, a staff
B) Silver pears
C) A ruby, a diamond, an emerald
D) Golden apples

Answer: D.
The eldest son collects all three golden apples for the princess.

33

Beauty and the Beast hails from what country?
A) France
B) Germany
C) England
D) Sweden

Answer: A.
Beauty and the Beast was written by a French Writer, Madame Gabrielle-Suzanne de Villeneuve in 1740.

34

Who published The Little Mermaid?
A) Charles Dickens
B) Hans Christian Anderson
C) Jeanette Hassenpflug
D) Charles Perrault

Answer: B.
Hans Christian Anderson also wrote The Princess and the Pea and The Ugly Duckling.

35

What does the second pig build his house of in the Three Little Pigs?
A) Straw
B) Wood
C) Paper
D) Bricks

Answer: B.
The Three Little Pigs is a fable about three pigs who build three houses of different materials. The first pig builds a house of straw, the second a house of wood, and the third makes a house of bricks.

36

Where is Rapunzel trapped by the witch?
A) A dungeon
B) A tower
C) A castle
D) A palace

Answer: B.
Rapunzel's Tower is where Rapunzel lived for 18 years.

37

Who gets Grandma out of the wolf's stomach in Little Red Riding Hood?
A) Grandpa
B) Little Red Riding Hood
C) The woodcutter
D) The forest animals

Answer: C.
The woodcutter kills the wolf with his axe and saves the grandmother.

38

What kind of animal was Abu in Aladdin?
A) Monkey
B) Tiger
C) Elephant
D) Bird

Answer: A.
Abu is Aladdin's pet monkey and friend, alongside Genie and Carpet.

FINAL WORDS

Thank you so much for taking the time to read my book!

I hope you enjoyed going through these trivia questions as much as I enjoyed scouring the globe to find them (trust me when I say it was a heck of an adventure).

I should note that it doesn't stop here.

I mean, you have this book forever – which means you can share them time and time again with all your friends and family.

What are you waiting for?

Get reading, get sharing, and most importantly, get thinking!

www.ingramcontent.com/pod-product-compliance
Lightning Source LLC
Chambersburg PA
CBHW071459070526
44578CB00001B/387